What's the State Legislative Branch?

Nancy Harris

Heinemann Library
Chicago, IL

©2008 Heinemann Library
a division of Reed Elsevier Inc.
Chicago, Illinois

Customer Service **888-454-2279**
Visit our website at **www.heinemannlibrary.com**

Photo research by Tracy Cummins and Tracey Engel
Designed by Kimberly R. Miracle and Betsy Wernert
Printed in China by South China Printing Company

11 10 09 08 07
10 9 8 7 6 5 4 3 2 1

ISBN-10:1-4034-9510-6 (hc)   1-4034-9516-5 (pb)

Library of Congress Cataloging-in-Publication Data
Harris, Nancy, 1956-
  What's the state legislative branch? / Nancy Harris.
     p. cm. -- (First guide to government)
  Includes bibliographical references and index.
  ISBN 978-1-4034-9510-5 (hc) -- ISBN 978-1-4034-9516-7 (pb)
  1. Legislative bodies--United States--States--Juvenile literature. I. Title.
  JK2488.H37 2007
  328.73--dc22

                    2007010916

Acknowledgments
The author and publishers are grateful to the following for permission to reproduce copyright material: ©age footstock **p. 12** (Dennis MacDonald); ©Alamy **p. 7** (Glow Images); ©Annapolis & Anne Arundel County Conference & Visitors Bureau **p. 6**; ©AP Photo **pp. 8** (Wide World Images), **10** (Gerry Broome), **11** (Harry Cabluck), **15** (Wide World Images), **16** (Wide World Images), **17** (Wide World Images), **18** (Wide World Images), **19** (Wide World Images) **20** (Wide World Images), **21** (Wide World Images), **23** (Wide World Images), **24** (Wide World Images), **25** (Wide World Images); ©CORBIS **p. 28** (SABA/ David Butow); ©Image Work **p. 9** (Jeff Greenberg); ©Landov **p. 26** (UPI /KEN JAMES); ©Map Resources **p. 4**; ©PhotoEdit Inc **p. 27** (Tom Carter); ©Regional Development Institute, Northern Illinois University **pp. 13, 14**; ©Super Stock **p. 29** (age footstock).

Cover photography reproduced with permission of AP Photo/Roberto Borea.

Every effort has been made to contact copyright holders of any material reproduced in this book. Any omissions will be rectified in subsequent printings if notice is given to the publisher.

Contents

Some words are shown in bold, **like this**. You can find out what they mean by looking in the glossary.

State Governments

Each state has its own government. The state government leads the whole state. The state government is made up of people who are **elected** (chosen) to run the state.

★ There are 50 states in the United States.

The state government is made up of three branches (parts). Each branch has a special job. One branch is called the state legislative branch.

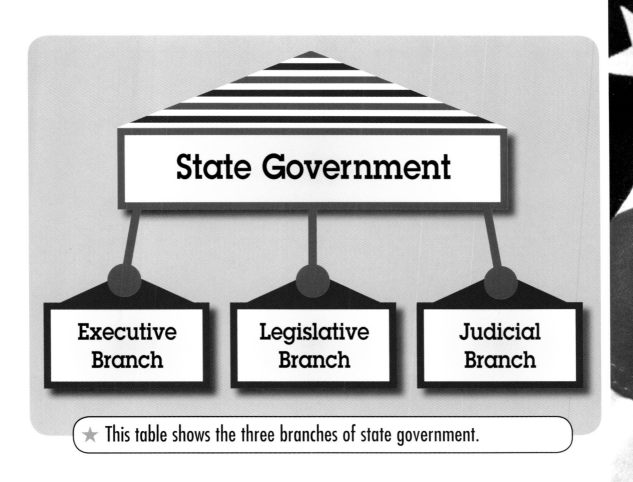

State Government

| Executive Branch | Legislative Branch | Judicial Branch |

★ This table shows the three branches of state government.

The State Legislative Branch

MARYLAND STATE HOUSE
BUILT 1772-1779
CAPITOL OF THE UNITED STATES
NOVEMBER 26, 1783 - AUGUST 13, 1784
IN THIS STATE HOUSE, OLDEST IN THE NATION STILL
IN LEGISLATIVE USE, GENERAL GEORGE WASHINGTON
RESIGNED HIS COMMISSION BEFORE THE CONTINENTAL
CONGRESS DECEMBER 23, 1783. HERE, JANUARY 14, 1784,
CONGRESS RATIFIED THE TREATY OF PARIS TO END THE
REVOLUTIONARY WAR AND, MAY 7, 1784, APPOINTED
THOMAS JEFFERSON MINISTER PLENIPOTENTIARY. FROM
HERE, SEPTEMBER 14, 1786, THE ANNAPOLIS CONVENTION
ISSUED THE CALL TO THE STATES THAT LED TO THE
CONSTITUTIONAL CONVENTION.

A REGISTERED NATIONAL HISTORIC LANDMARK
MARYLAND HISTORICAL SOCIETY

★★★ People in the state legislative branch work
in the state Capitol building.

People who work in the state legislative branch make
laws (rules) for the state. These laws help run the state.

6

States can make their own laws. They must also follow the laws of the United States **federal government**. The federal government makes decisions for the entire country.

Washington, D.C.

★ The United States federal government is in Washington, D.C.

People who work in the state legislative branch are called state legislators. They present ideas for new **laws**. They vote for new laws.

★ State legislators discuss possible laws for the state.

★ Citizens vote to elect their state leaders.

In most states, the legislative branch is divided into two groups of people. These groups are called the upper house and the lower house.

The people in each house are **elected** by **citizens** in the state. Citizens are people who can vote for leaders to represent them.

The Upper House

Every state except Nebraska has an upper house in the **legislative branch**. The upper house is called the **Senate**. In most states, people in the upper house serve longer than people in the lower house.

★★★ This is where the upper house meets in the state of North Carolina.

People who work in the state Senate are called senators. Each senator represents the same number of people in the state.

★ These are state senators from Texas.

The Lower House

Every state except Nebraska has a lower house in the **legislative branch**. In most states, this house is called the **House of Representatives**. People who work in this house are called representatives.

This is a photograph of the lower house in the state of Michigan.

Making State Laws

★ Anyone in the state can come up with an idea for a state law.

Both houses of the state legislative branch are involved in making state **laws**. First someone comes up with an idea for a state law. Then a state legislator writes a report about the idea.

The report is called a **bill**. The bill is brought to the state legislative branch by a legislator. The legislator can be a member of the upper or lower house.

★ Members of the state legislature discuss bills in meetings.

★ A bill is reviewed by all of the state legislators.

In most states, one house reads the bill first. People in that house have many discussions and meetings about the bill.

★ Legislators vote to decide if a bill should become a **law**.

Then people in that house vote on the **bill**. If most people vote for the bill, it is sent to the other house. The second house in the state legislative branch then looks at the bill.

This house also holds many discussions and meetings. The second house then votes to decide if the bill should become a law.

★★★ Legislators in the second house discuss the bill before voting on it.

If most people in the second house vote for the **bill**, it is sent to the **governor**. The governor is the leader of the state. If the governor signs the bill, it becomes a state **law**.

★ The governor is the leader of a state government.

Making the State Budget

People in the state legislative branch help make the **budget** for their state. The budget is a list of how much money is needed to run each part of the state government. Each state decides on its own budget needs.

★ This legislator is reading about his state's budget.

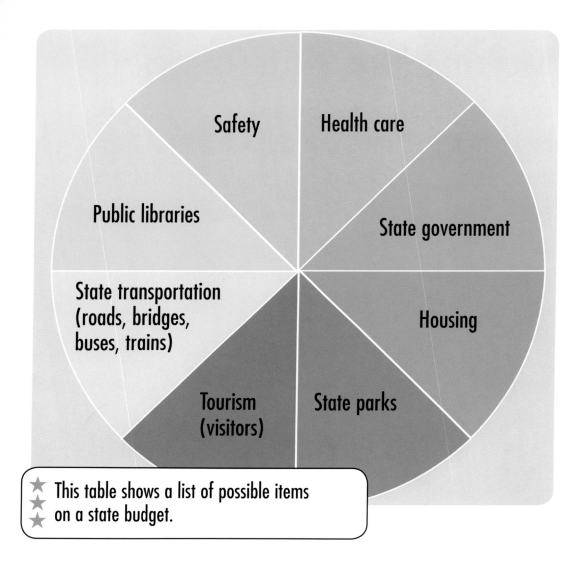

Safety

Health care

Public libraries

State government

State transportation
(roads, bridges,
buses, trains)

Housing

Tourism
(visitors)

State parks

★★★ This table shows a list of possible items
on a state budget.

The **budget** money is used to run state **departments**. These are groups of people who help run the state. Some money may go toward the department in charge of repairing highways and bridges. It could also be used to build new schools and hospitals.

In some states, the **governor** suggests the state budget plan. He or she presents the budget to state legislators.

★ Governors may present the budget to the press.

★
★
★ People in both houses meet together to discuss the budget.

After the **governor** presents the **budget**, it is discussed by state legislators. It can also be discussed in meetings by the state's **citizens**.

★ These legislators are voting on their state's budget.

State legislators must vote to **approve** the budget.
They read the budget and decide if they agree with it.
If they vote in favor of the budget, it is put into effect.

★★★ Governor Schwarzenegger of California is signing the state budget.

In some states, legislators create the **budget**. Then they vote to **approve** it. If most legislators vote for the budget, it is sent to the **governor**. If the governor signs it, the budget is approved.

Who Can Serve as State Legislator?

★★★ People running for state legislator meet with citizens to hear their concerns.

There are **laws** that say who can serve in the **s**tate legislative branch. In all states, legislators must be U.S. **citizens**. They must live in their **district** for a certain period of time. They must also be a certain age.

In most states, people in the upper house serve a **term** of four years. People in the lower house usually serve a term of two years. Legislators can be **elected** again by the state's **citizens**. In many states, there is no limit to how many times they can be elected.

★ Citizens vote for their state legislators.

Making Laws for Our States

The state legislative branch is an important part of the state government. This branch makes state **laws**. The laws are made for the good of the people in the state.

WYOMING STATE CAPITOL

Glossary

approve agree to

bill written idea for a new law

budget list of money needed to run each part of the state government

citizen person who is born in the United States. People who have moved to the United States from another country can become citizens by taking a test.

department group of people who help run the state. Each department has a specific job.

district area in a state

elect choose a leader by voting

federal government group of leaders who run the country. In a federal government, the country is made up of many states.

governor leader of a state. The governor works in the state executive branch.

House of Representatives lower house in the state legislative branch. In some states, it is called the Assembly or the House of Delegates.

law rule people must obey in a state or country

population number of people who live in an area

Senate upper house in the state legislative branch

term length of time a leader serves in a position

More Books to Read

De Capua, Sarah. *Making a Law.* New York: Children's Press, 2004.

Firestone, Mary. *The State Legislative Branch.* Mankato, MN: Capstone Press, 2004.

Web Sites

Great Government for Kids has information about local government, state governments, and the federal government.
http://www.cccoe.net/govern/index.html

Visit PBS Kids' the Democracy Project to play fun games and learn all about how local, state, and federal governments run your city or town.
http://pbskids.org/democracy/mygovt/police.html

Index